YOU CAN'T DO BUSINESS

(or Most Anything Else)

WITHOUT YIDDISH

YOU CAN'T DO BUSINESS
(or Most Anything Else)
WITHOUT YIDDISH

by

LEON H. GILDIN
(LEIBLE)

Illustrations by

PAUL PETER PORGES
(P.P.P.)

HIPPOCRENE BOOKS, INC.
NEW YORK

Copyright©2000 Leon H. Gildin

ISBN 0-7818-0818-9

For information, address:
HIPPOCRENE BOOKS, INC.
171 Madison Avenue
New York, NY 10016

Cataloging-in-Publication Data available from the Library of Congress

Printed in the United States of America.

Dedication

Not a sentence, an expression, or a word in this book could be written without mention of the role played by my long departed parents, Grisha (Harry) and Ida Gildin,. "Olev hasholam" (may they rest in peace).

Their love and continued devotion to the Yiddish language combined with their Americanization (my father met my mother on the first day of his arrival in the United States in 1912) acted as a lifelong inspiration to my brothers and to me.

To write a book such as this and not give my parents the "kovid" (credit) due to them would be a "shanda" (shame).

Leible

Acknowledgements

I must give both credit and thanks in the creation of this book to my beloved wife, Gloria. Although her knowledge of Yiddish was very limited, she spent the last year reading books, magazines, and newspapers with a pad and pencil by her side and each time she came upon a Yiddish word, she'd ask, "How about this one? Do you have it?" You'd be surprised how many words she found.

Thanks to Lois Kane in Sedona, Arizona for reading my handwriting, secretarial services and believe it or not, even a word or two from the old days. (Who knew she was Jewish?)

A special thanks to my agent, Jane Dystel of Jane Dystel Literary Management, Inc. She taught me how to create a presentation (always start with a joke) and no matter how much I argued and fought, she insisted that she was right. Guess what? She was.

And last but by no means least, my editors, Nadia Hassani and Carol Chitnis, who raised issues, asked questions, but even more than I, sought perfection. For that I thank them and will always be grateful.

Table of Contents

Introduction

To understand its depth and beauty, readers should recognize that Yiddish is a full and complete language with a distinct grammar, a voluminous literature and a rich history. Germanic in origin, it is estimated to be 1,000 years old, (celebrating its millennium), and as the Jews wandered, particularly through Eastern Europe, the language took on localisms and foreign words of the countries in which the people settled. In addition, local areas produced local dialects, the principal ones being Lithuanian, Polish, Ukrainian, and Galician. As a result, one Jew meeting another was always able to tell what part of the country was home to a visitor.

In addition to local words, expressions and dialect, many Hebrew words and expressions found their way into the language. Certain Hebrew words are accepted as absolutes in Yiddish such as "Yom Tov" meaning "holiday" (literally translated as "day good" or figuratively as a good day), Saturday or the Sabbath is "Shabbos" (Ashkenazi) or "Shabbat" (Sephardic).

Certain words, both Hebrew and German, are acceptable usage in Yiddish. War, for instance, is the Hebrew word "milchoma," however, the German word "krieg" is permissible in Yiddish. Peace, as we all know, is "shalom" but the word "frieden" is also a synonym in

Yiddish. On the other hand, truth is "emes" (Hebrew), and although there is a German word for truth, it is never used in Yiddish.

If there was ever a universal language, Yiddish would have to be on top of the list. Moving from country to country, whether by choice or by compulsion, Yiddish accompanied the traveler. When a thousand or more miles from home, a Jew heard a word of "mame-loshn," the mother tongue, he knew he was amongst "landsman," compatriots.

The severest blow to Yiddish was, of course, World War II and the Holocaust. The six million Jews who died in the Nazi extermination camps were almost all Yiddish speaking and their loss, both to the language and to the world, is inestimable and irreplaceable.

How interesting it is to find that a country like Australia reversed the procedure and incorporated Yiddish words into its slang vocabulary. "Shikker" and "shikkered," meaning drunk or what you do when you go out on the town. "Cobber," meaning mate or pal, coming from "chaver" and a little girl is known as a "clinah" from the Yiddish "kleine," meaning small.

Similarly, Jewish immigration to the United States over the last 100 years, particularly from Eastern Europe, and the involvement of these new Americans in the commercial and artistic life of this country, has resulted in Yiddish assuming an important place in the everyday language of commerce and business as well as family life. In order to make a deal, you have to "handl" or negotiate and when the deal is done, especially in the diamond trade, the parties, not only Jews, shake hands and say, "mazl un brocha," luck and blessing.

I am hopeful that *You Can't Do Business ...* will appeal to both the Jewish and non-Jewish reader. In a recent book, *Master of Dreams: A Memoir of Isaac Bashevis Singer* by Dvorah Telushkin, published by William Morrow (1998), there is a list of forty-six Yiddish words, many of them found in *You Can't Do Business ...* which have already been incorporated into English and appear in Webster's Third New International Dictionary.

Despite the incorporation of Yiddish into the English language, there has been a great revival of interest in Yiddish in the last decade as is evidenced by the number of colleges and universities that are teaching the language. Prior to this revival, the language had fallen into disuse except among orthodox Jews who used Yiddish as their everyday means of discourse. Hebrew was only for prayer and was called "loshn kodesh," a holy language never to be used for business or family matters.

Most second and third generation Jews found that their use of Yiddish was limited to what they remembered from their grandparents or what comics used in their Borscht Belt routines. Jews reading *You Can't Do Business ...* will hopefully learn a few new/old words or expressions but will certainly enjoy being reminded of what was once a meaningful and familiar part of their lives. Non-Jews, on the other hand, upon reading *You Can't Do Business ...* will suddenly become aware of how much Yiddish they see in their daily newspapers, magazines, movies and television. There is rarely an article or a TV show dealing with the big city or the police that does not incorporate a Yiddish expression or curse word. The most remarkable part of this is that the non-Jew knows and understands the words or expressions but, in many instances is not aware that it comes from Yiddish.

A political cartoon appearing in the Sunday New York Times on July 11, 1999 depicted Hillary Clinton in pursuit of her nomination for the Senate. It is a four panel cartoon and the last two panels read: A REGULAR YANKEE ROOTING CHUTZPAH-HAVING NEW YORKER—A REGULAR YANKEE ROOTING CHUTZPAH-HAVING, CARPETBAG SCHLEPPING NEW YORKER.

Since Mrs. Clinton is seeking the Jewish vote in New York, the words Chutzpah-Having and Carpetbag-Schlepping are in heavy print, thereby, making what is an obvious point. The New York Times, by the very use of the words "chutzpah" (nerve) and "schlepping" (dragging or pulling), presupposes that non-Jews, as well, know the meaning of these words and will see the humor in the cartoon. Curse words such as "putz" or "schmuck" (both referring to penis but having other meanings as well) are further examples of Yiddish words used by non-Jews in ordinary conversation, but may not realize that they are Yiddish in origin.

There can be no question that the Jewish upbringing of the comedians who played the Catskill hotels, the nightclubs in their heyday, and ultimately Broadway, Hollywood, and TV meant that Yiddish words and expressions were intimately entwined in their routines. Could Myron Cohen tell a story about the Garment Center on the Ed Sullivan Show without using Yiddish? Could Jackie Mason be appreciated without knowing some Yiddish? Just recently on a popular police drama on TV, the black lieutenant referred to the party to be arrested as a "zhlub" (a yokel, a boor, or a dumb ox), a word clearly found in Weinreich's English/Yiddish dictionary.

I sincerely trust that you will read and enjoy *You Can't Do Business (Or Most Anything Else) Without Yiddish* and, above all, understand why it was important for the book to be written. The Yiddish speaking immigrant in America was both a religious and secular force in Jewish life for close to 100 years. The Yiddish press published more newspapers than any other foreign language daily. The Yiddish theater had more theaters and productions than any other immigrant group and sent more actors and actresses from the Yiddish stage to Hollywood than any other foreign language troupe. The secular Yiddish speaking world had elementary and high schools, publishing houses, summer camps, literary groups and fraternal orders. As a result, they exerted a cultural dominance rarely seen in an immigrant society.

I hope, therefore, that *You Can't Do Business ...* will remain a small part of the world that was and the world that may yet be.

Leon H. Gildin
(Leible)

The Garment Center

As the Yiddish speaking immigration from Eastern Europe grew, the immigrants' means of livelihood in the "old country" played an important role in naming them here in America. The "chazzan" became Cantor, the shoemaker called himself Shuster, the storekeeper chose Kramer, the one who made "challah" for the Sabbath was called Baker or Becker, the scribe was Schreiber, and the tailor was called Schneider.

The tailors now divided themselves up by their specialties. In 1900, those who worked in the manufacture of dresses and blouses formed the International Ladies Garment Workers Union. This was almost exclusively an east coast occupation in which both men and women worked in "sweat shops," under incredibly unsanitary and hazardous conditions. Average wages were from $7.00 to $11.00 per week for workdays of sixteen hours or more. At the time the union was formed, some 84,000 men and women were engaged in the ladies' needle trade.

The men's needle trade, on the other hand, was both organized and disorganized from the 1880s on. It was a more widespread industry and there were general strikes in New York, Chicago, and elsewhere in the United States between 1880 and 1914. Ultimately, in Nashville, Tennessee in 1914, the Amalgamated Clothing Workers of America was formed and due to the government not wishing unfavorable publicity with respect to the manufacture of uniforms during World

War I, the union was successful in eliminating "sweat shop" conditions and child labor. By the end of the war, the union had reduced the work week to 48 hours and by January 1919 it was further reduced to 44 hours.

The Garment Center itself is an area in New York City which incorporates both men's and women's needle trades and extends from 14ᵀᴴ Street to 40ᵀᴴ Street. Also encompassed by these blocks are the related manufacture of furs, notions and trimmings, and millinery. The industries have their own restaurants, both "milchiks," (dairy) and "fleischiks" (meat based), kosher and non-kosher, and their own synagogues. The Garment Center has always added a distinct flavor to the ethnic mix of New York.

An interesting aside is that the Italian immigrant population also worked in the garment industry and in many instances, were under the direction of Jewish foorepersons or bosses. As a result, as the industry and the workers became Americanized, you had non-Jews continuing to use the Yiddish expressions which were accepted as the language of the industry.

GELT	Money, folding green; what's necessary to guarantee that next year's line will be out on time.
GLITZY	Shiny, sparkling and glittery; what looks good on the runway model who is 5'10" tall and weighs 110 lbs.
KHAZERAY	Junk; what the competition manufactures.
MAZOOMA	From the Hebrew, Mizoomin, meaning cash. No matter what language, it's still "gelt" and is what's needed to buy the overruns for the discount stores.
NACHES	Pride, pleasure, special joy; the feeling the designer expresses to his models, his tailors, and all the others who made the show the success that it was.
SCHLOCK	A cheap or inferior line made by a schlock house.
SCHMALTZY	Derived from chicken fat. Sexy, low cut, glitzy and generally in poor taste.
SCHNEIDER	Literally a cutter; generally speaking, a tailor.
SHLEPPER	One who drags; the kid who pushes the hand-truck on 7ᵀᴴ Avenue.

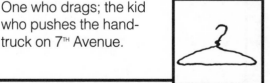

GLITZY

Shiny, sparkling and glittery; what looks good on the runway model who is 5'10" tall and weighs 110 lbs.

SHMATTE	A rag; but the industry is known worldwide as the "shamatte business" even in the ateliers of Paris.
SHNITZY	Definitely upper crust; most of us can only afford the knockoffs.
TACHLIS	Results; brass tacks. I'm the boss and what I say goes. I want results.

SHLEPPER

One who drags; the kid who pushes the handtruck on 7TH Avenue.

One day, God came to a "shtetl" in Eastern Europe to observe the meticulous work of a "schneider" who was making a "kapote" or caftan for the Rabbi. God was so impressed that he made himself known to the "schneider," expressed admiration for his work, and suggested that they go into business together.

The "schneider" was overwhelmed at the idea of being in business with God and said, "But how can I be in business with God? What will we call the business?"

God thought for a moment and said, "I have it. How about Lord & Taylor?"

Misunderstandings are always good for a joke.

Jake, a cutter by dresses, went out for lunch and while walking to the restaurant, was struck by a "shlepper" pulling a loaded handtruck. Murphy, the cop on the beat, saw Jake lying on the sidewalk in pain, called EMS and helped lift Jake onto the gurney.

"Are you comfortable?" Murphy asked.

"Danks God, I make a living," Jake replied.

Food,
Restaurants
and Catering

Restaurants and Catering services developed around those businesses and industries in which Jews predominated. As a result, many delicacies retained their original Yiddish name and a "Yiddishn tam" (a Jewish flavor). Menus were printed in Yiddish or in transliteration, and the "old country" identification kept the customer happy. Jewish "simchas" (happy events), and even Jewish funerals created a demand for catering services, and to this day the fanciest of Jewish caterers will feature delicacies by using the original Yiddish name or description of the food.

Just as they had their own languages, Jews from various parts of the world had their own regional specialties, as well as different names for the same food. Sephardim, Jews who came from Spain and the Mediterranean countries, use lamb and rice as staples of their diet. These foods, although known to the Ashkenazi Jews, are rarely part of the Northern European diet and are considered much more Oriental in nature.

The popular Yiddish song, "ROUMANIA" speaks of a "carnatzl" (sausage), a "pastraml" (pastrami) "un a glezele vien" (and a glass of wine). Obviously, a local combination of delicacies.

Among the wealthier Jews of Germany, a typical side dish was a "kartoffel," (potato). To the poorer Jews of Eastern Europe, it was known as a "bulba" and unfortunately, as is sung in the song "BULBAS," it was the entire meal for the whole week until Shabbos. Then they made a "bulbele kigele" (a diminutive potato pudding), only to return to "bulbas" for the new week.

We are all familiar with blintzes. They can be made from scratch or purchased in the frozen food section of any supermarket. I had a mother-in-law who came from the Ukraine who referred to them as "melintzes." I had never heard the word and in checking it out with authorities, I was told that it is not an uncommon usage by people from that certain area.

So, as with any other business, it appears that the defining element for Food, Restaurants and Catering is: location, location, location.

A GLEZELE TAY / MIT TZUKER / MIT VARENYA	A glass (diminutive) of tea / With sugar. (For the old timers, it was a sugar cube held between the teeth.) / With cherry preserves.
BAGEL	By this time, it should be universally known as a Jewish donut; however, I heard that when a Midwesterner visiting New York was offered a bagel and cream cheese, his only question was: which is the bagel and which is the cream cheese?
BIALY	A baked roll/bagel supposed to have originated in Bialostok, in the Ukraine.
BLINTZES	Thin layers of dough filled with cheese or potatoes, fried and usually eaten with smetana (sour cream).
BORSCHT	Beet soup in the summer with a boiled potato and sour cream; cabbage soup in the winter, sometimes with flanken (short ribs) or sometimes with sour cream.
BROIT	Bread; for weekdays.

CHALLAH	Leavened egg bread for shabbos and Yom-Tov.
CHALUPCHES / PROKES	Meat rolled in cabbage; usually in sweet and sour gravy.
CHAMETZ	Leavened bread; food prohibited on Passover.
CHAZZER	Pig; ham or bacon. Definitely a no-no if you are Kosher.
CHOLNT	A mixture of meat, vegetables and potatoes prepared on Friday by Orthodox Jews and kept warm for eating on the Sabbath.
CHRAIN	Horseradish, red or white, good on flanken or gefilte fish, but too much will clear your sinuses.
FEIG	A fig; also used as an expression of disrespect when one puts one's thumb between the second and third finger and holds it up to someone.
FLANKEN	Short ribs of beef; boiled or in soup, delicious with chrain.

FLEISCHIK	Meat based.
GEFILTE FISH	A combination of carp and whitefish ground up, rolled up into balls and boiled. From the jar, it's edible; when homemade for Passover, it's delicious but don't forget the chrain.
GEHAKTE LEBER	Chopped liver. (It has also come to mean something derogatory or trivial; So what am I …?)
GRIVENESS	Chicken skin fried in "schmaltz" and eaten with onions, a white radish and hard-boiled eggs. (Oh, boy, is that good but what it does to your cholesterol is not to be talked about.)
GRUBBE ZALTZ	Thick salt or Kosher salt.
HALVAH	A Turkish confection of sesame seeds and honey. When covered with milk chocolate, it's a real "meichel" (taste treat).
HAMANTASCHEN	A three-cornered cookie dough filled with poppy seeds, prunes or apricots. A special treat during Purim.

GEFILTE FISH

A combination of carp and whitefish ground up, rolled up into balls and boiled. From the jar, it's edible; when homemade for Passover, it's delicious but don't forget the chrain.

HELZL / GERGL	The neck of a chicken.
KARTOFFEL / BULBAS	Potatoes, depending upon where you come from.
KASHA	Buckwheat groats; a cereal product very often mixed with fried onions, chicken fat or other delicacies.
KASHA VARNICHKES	Groats and noodles (bowties); a side dish with flanken and gravy.
KATCHKE	Duck.
KISHKA	Stuffed derma (intestines).
KNAIDLACH	Matzoh balls; soft like squeezing a baby's cheek or hard for throwing at your enemies.
KNISH	Dough wrapped around potatoes or kasha. (It also has a dirty meaning.)
KOSHER	Meeting Biblical Jewish standards of purity; Rabbinically approved.
KREPLACH	Jewish won-ton; a holiday "meichel."
KUGEL	Or depending on where you came from KIGEL; a noodle "pudjing" sweet with raisins for some, salt and pepper for others.

LATKES	Holiday pancakes of potatoes or matzo meal, especially for Channukah; sometimes served with powdered sugar, applesauce or "smetana" (sour cream).
LEKAKH	Honey cake.
LEKVAR	Prune butter.
LOKSCHN	Noodles.
MANDLIN	Dry soup nuts or almonds.
MATZOHS	Unleavened bread; a must at Passover but good all year round.
MATZOH BREI	Matzohs, softened in hot water, dipped in egg and fried.
MATZOH MEAL	Matzohs reduced to flour for breading, baking or making "knaidlach".
MILCHIK	Milk based.
MILTZ	Spleen.

NOSH	A snack of any or all of these goodies, especially between meals. Good with coffee or tea.
PAREVE	Neither milchiks nor fleischiks.
PIROGEN / PIROSCHKE	Russian/Polish dish. Dough (like won-ton) filled with cheese, meat or potatoes; boiled or fried.
PITCHA	Jellied calves feet.
PULKE	Chicken thigh.
PUPIK	Belly button; a part of the innards of a chicken.
RUGELACH	Tasty little fruitcakes, appropriate when paying a "shiva" (condolence) call.
RUSL	Beet juice; pickle juice.
SCHMALTZ	Chicken fat; from the word "schmaltzen," to melt or to render; with "grubbe zalts," kosher salt, on rye bread; a real "meichel."
SCHMIER	Two inches of cream cheese on a bagel; literally to paint or to spread.
SCHNAPPS	An alcoholic drink like Old Overholt.

HELZL, GERGL

The neck of a chicken.

SCHNITZEL — Meat dipped in egg and bread crumbs or matzoh meal and fried in oil.

SHPRITZER — White wine and seltzer; one who squirts.

SHTICKEL — A small piece; years ago hard salami was sold for a nickel a shtickel, and if you were nice, the deli-man would throw in a pickle.

SMETANA — A Czech composer but more familiarly, sour cream; for borscht, for latkes, for blintzes, and even for cottage cheese.

STRUDEL — Flaky dough with fruit or nuts.

TAIGLACH — Dry balls of cake in honey with maraschino cherries.

TAM — Taste.

TAM GAN-AIDEN — The taste of the garden of Eden.

TRAIF — Not kosher; a no-no.

TSIBBELE — An onion; preferably the kind that makes you cry when you slice it.

TSIMMES

Carrots with sugar or honey, or sweet carrots with meat or potatoes; sweet potatoes, prunes and apricots or any other combination resulting in a sweet side dish; so many different mixtures that it has come to mean a "to-do" over anything.

KNAIDLACH

Matzoh balls; soft like squeezing a baby's cheek or hard for throwing at your enemies.

Jewish food has always been a source of humor. One can never forget the story told by Buddy Hackett about his reaction to eating army food. He baffled the doctors on sick call when he complained that without the "chrain" (horseradish), the "shamaltz" (chicken fat), and the "tsibbeles" (onions), the heartburn necessary to life was no more. The fire had gone out.

The eternal conflict between the Jewish waiter and his customer was never expressed as eloquently as in the following story:

After being served a steaming bowl of chicken soup by a waiter in a typically Jewish delicatessen, the customer, realizing he had no soup spoon, asked the waiter to taste the soup. "Vos iz?" (What is it?) asked the waiter. "Just taste the soup," said the customer. "Farvoss?" (Why?) asked the waiter. "Just taste it," repeated the frustrated customer. With great annoyance, the waiter said, "Nu, vu is dos lefl?" (Well, where is the spoon?) "Aha," said the customer, victoriously.

So the reader should not say, "Aha, something is missing," here are the implements needed both at home and in a restaurant.

1. Gluz	A Glass
2. Gupl	A Fork
3. Lefl	A Spoon
4. Messer	A Knife
5. Servetke or Serviet	A Napkin
6. Teller	A Plate
7. Tishtach	A Tablecloth

And from the "bubbe's tzeitn" (grandma's time)

8. Bretl	A Board for rolling dough.
9. Kokhlefl	A mixing spoon; a yenta who gets involved in everybody's business.
10. Valgerholz	A rolling pin; literally, a roaming piece of wood.

Now you tell me: Where would the expression "Eat your heart out" come from, if not from Jewish cooking?

Show Biz

Along with the carpenters (Stollers), tailors (Schneiders) and shoemakers (Shusters) who came to the United States in and around the turn of the century, Eastern Europe and Germany exported many playwrights, actors, singers and others who had worked in the theater. These immigrants became, not only the basis for the Yiddish Theater in New York (Jacob Adler, Molly Picon, Maurice Schwartz, Paul Muni, etc.), but founded the movie industry in Hollywood, became popular as comedians and singers on radio and television and are acknowledged to have contributed greatly to the development of the many faceted gem known as show business.

Jewish playwrights of renown have been active since the end of the American Revolution and remain in the forefront of theater up to the present day. Children of immigrants who won Pulitzer prizes and Drama Critics Awards from the 1920's to the 1940's included Elmer Rice, George S. Kaufman, Sidney Kingsley, and Lillian Hellman. Popular playwrights of today include Neil Simon, David Mamet, Arthur Miller, Israel Horovitz and many others.

Where there were playwrights, there were musicals. Although the music was original, much of the work of first generation composers incorporated both popular melodies of the "shtetl" and liturgical themes of the synagogue. Prize winning composers and lyricists who have become household names in America include Irving Berlin (Israel

Baline), Harold Arlen (Hyman Arluck), George Gershwin (Jacob Gershwine), as well as Rodgers & Hart, Sigmund Romberg, and Jerome Kern.

Comics, almost too numerous to mention, started in the late 1800's with Weber and Fields. Combining comedy with music gave us vaudeville and burlesque, and along came Al Jolson, Eddie Cantor, George Jessel, Bert Lahr, Milton Berle, and Danny Kaye. Fanny Brice was the outstanding musical comedienne and, last but not least, the Marx Brothers, who made their name in vaudeville, went on to the fast rising motion picture business in Hollywood.

After World War II, the Catskill Mountains became the vacation spot for Jews who sought relief from the tumult of New York. Bungalow colonies for the families in the summer, and hotels year round for the more upscale guests who couldn't do without three meals a day. Grossinger's, The Concord, Brown's, and The Nevele became show places for Jewish comedians. After the ten o'clock show ended at the hotels, the twelve o'clock show would begin in the casinos at the bungalow colonies.

Affectionately known as the Borscht Belt, the Catskills was home to stars such as Jerry Lewis, Red Buttons, Sid Caesar, Milton Berle, Henny Youngman, Myron Cohen, Morey Amsterdam, Sam Levinson, and Alan King. A good part of their humor was based on their families, their background and their employment—always centered on the Jewish ethnic experience.

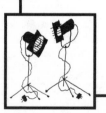

As far as singers are concerned, well-known opera stars such as Jan Peerce and Robert Merrill performed and recorded both liturgical music and Yiddish folk music. More recent performers who have continued this tradition and can now be found on CDs are Barbra Streisand and Mandy Patinkin.

Certain radio stations in the big cities always had Yiddish programming, particularly on Sunday. Inevitably, radio and television started to include Jewish characters in both comedy and drama who were, in many instances, portrayed as neurotic and stereotypic. Research has shown, however, that Jewish themes have become more prevalent on TV as is demonstrated by the information contained in the scholarly work, *The Chosen Image: Television's Portrayal of Jewish Themes and Characters,* by Jonathan and Judith Pearl. The Pearls have catalogued five decades of prime-time Jewish content and organized them into six major categories: Rites and Rituals, Encountering America, Anti-Semitism, The Holocaust, Israel, and Intermarriage. A 1991 script of "The Simpsons," a cartoon program, quoted a line from a book by Sammy Davis, Jr., entitled: *Yes, I Can.* "The Jews are a swinging bunch of people," he said.

Taking all things into consideration, the Jewish/Yiddish contribution to show biz was enormous.

BORSCHT BELT	The Catskill Mountains—each hotel served its own beet soup in the summer and cabbage soup in the winter, and from out of the soup came some of America's most renowned comics.
CHAZZAN	Cantor. Although their principal function was as interpreters of liturgical music, chazzunim (plural) were also some of the greatest singers of Yiddish folk music. The story of a chazzan and his son became the inspiration for the first talking film, *The Jazz Singer* with Al Jolson.
DREI-BUCH	A script; the cameraman turned the film by hand.
DREI-KOP	Someone who makes you crazy with a new plot for the movie, a new deal with the producer, etc.
FREILACHS	A happy tune, based primarily on the folk music of the Chasidim in Poland and Galicia.

GANTZE MACHER	Literally, a big maker or doer; the CEO; a hotshot.
GLITZY	The look of a Las Vegas showgirl. Showy or gaudy; sure to catch the attention of the big spender.
GROISER KNOCKER	A big shot, at least so he believes.
GROISER KOKKER	A bullshit artist; your agent who promises, promises but never comes through.
HORA	A circle dance popularized in Israel and a favorite at all weddings and Bar Mitzvahs.
KAPPELYE	A folk band.
KITSCH	Gaudy, pretentious and shallow but with popular appeal.
KLEZMER	The musicians who were hired for weddings to play a "freilachs."
MEGILLAH	Historically and biblically the Story of Esther (Purim); a long drawn out account by your agent of why you didn't get the part.

GROISER KNOCKER

A big shot, at least so he believes.

MISHMASH	An unwieldy combination; if we combine the characters from Script A with the story from Script B; it usually doesn't work.
NIGN	A melody without words, of Chassidic origin.
NUSAKH	Traditional melodic patterns of prayers.
SCHLOCK MEISTER	A movie maker who produces kitsch.
SCHMALTZY	Highly sentimental, banal. "Her face was glued to the window as she watched (sob) (sob) . . ." but it's still derived from chicken fat.
SHPIEL	In the theater a "shpiel" is a play (drama).
SHTICK	Stuff or tricks; an individual's stock-in-trade.
TUMMLER	A noise-maker; if Buddy Hackett is at your party, you've definitely got one.

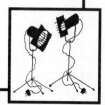

MISHMASH

An unwieldy combination; if we combine the characters from Script A with the story from Script B; it usually doesn't work.

SONGS

Bei Mir Bistu Schoen—To me you are beautiful; written originally for the Yiddish theater in 1932. Many years later new lyrics in English were written for the rest of the song but the first line remained in Yiddish. The original lyrics were:

> "Bei Mir Bistu Schoen, Bei Mir Hustu Chain."
> (To me you are beautiful; To me you have charm.)

The new lyrics were:

> "Bei Mir Bistu Schoen, Please let me explain. . . ."

A big hit for the Andrew Sisters in English and for the Barry (Begelman) Sisters in Yiddish.

Di Greine Kuzine—The green cousin; the word green being a slang shortening of greenhorn (an immigrant). Again, for the purposes of the rhyme, translating the Yiddish into English the first two lines are:

> "To me came a 'kuzine,'
> Beautiful as gold, was she the 'greine.'"

Rozhinkes mit Mandlen—Raisins and Almonds; a popular lullaby from the Yiddish Theater on Second Avenue in New York.

Shayne vi di Levune—Beautiful as the moon; a song of thanks by a boy for having received a girl whom he describes as a gift from heaven.

Yosl-Yosl—Joey, Joey. Originally in Yiddish then rewritten in English (not translated), in which a girl asks Joey to make his mind up and name the day. Another big hit for the Andrews Sisters.

My Yiddishe Mamma—A song recognized by audiences worldwide and originally made popular by Sophie Tucker in both Yiddish and English. (I personally heard it played by a band in the Borghese Gardens in Rome.)

In the 1930s and 40s, as a result of the success of "Bei Bei Mir Bistu Schoen," Tin Pan Alley couldn't get enough of Jewish music from the "shtetl." Cab Callaway discovered "Ut a Zoy Nayt a Schneider" (That's how a tailor sews) and recorded it under the title "Utt-Da-Zoy." Ziggy Elman, a trumpeter with Benny Goodman, found an old "klezmer" tune, renamed it "Freilach (happy) in Swing" and recorded it under the title of "And the Angels Sing."

Many other songs from the Second Avenue Yiddish theater had brief revivals but in the end, the use of this material was a short-lived fad.

Cops and Robbers (Gangster Talk)

At the end of the 19ᵀᴴ century, the port of Odessa in Crimea was totally controlled by Jewish longshoremen. No cargo could be loaded or unloaded without the "approval" of the bosses and any attempt at interference was dealt with with a strong right arm.

Out of the poverty and slums of the immigration of the early 20ᵀᴴ century came the Jewish gangster, whose religion and ethnic background played an interesting role in his chosen profession. From running numbers to murder, the Jewish gangster was prominent, particularly during the 20s, 30s, and 40s.

On one hand, Jewish factory owners hired Jewish gangsters to smash Jewish unions (schlamming ... wielding an iron pipe wrapped in newspaper). On the other hand, Red Levine refused to kill on Shabbos and Mickey Cohen could be counted on to beat up American Nazis as an act of charity. It is also alleged that Meyer Lansky, at the whispered request of Jewish leaders, rounded up enough thugs to break up a pro-Nazi rally.

Dutch Schultz (Arnold Flegenheimer) and his chief lieutenant Bo Weinberg were two of the biggest transporters of whiskey during prohibition. Louis (Lepke) Buchhalter, the prominent head of Murder, Inc., got his name from the fact that in Yiddish, Louis was Leible; as a child his mother called him "Leibke" a diminutive, and the rest of the world came to know him as Lepke.

No list of Jewish gangsters would be complete without mention of one of the Depression's most lethal mobsters, Abe (Kid Twist) Reles. Abe became a "shtinker" (read on and you'll learn what it means) and despite the protective custody of New York's Finest, his violent rise to fame was followed by an equally violent fall from the sixth floor of the Half-Moon Hotel in Coney Island, N.Y. Tabloid journalists of the day referred to him as "the canary who could sing but couldn't fly."

Sometimes an individual's name told the whole story. As a kid, he was such a "nudnik" (pest) that adults screamed at Jake Shapiro, "garratahere" (get out of here). As a mobster, he went through life with the name Garrah Shapiro or Jake Garrah.

Despite their livelihood, Jewish mobsters would not abandon Jewish family tradition. It is reported that the elite of Jewish gangsterism all gathered on the Lower East Side of New York to celebrate the "bris" (circumcision) of Charlie (the Bug) Workman's son, Solomon. For some reason, the immorality of their lives played no role in their desire to observe their upbringing and the practices of their religion.

Although the Jewish gangster worked hand in hand with Italian crime families, their ultimate interests were not the same. The Jewish gangster took no pride in seeing to

it that his children became part of the family "business." The children represented the American dream: going off to college to become doctors, lawyers and businessmen.

The gangsterism of the father was a means to an end and once the end was achieved, and the second and third generations became Americanized, most of the Jewish gangsters disappeared.

FIN (English)	A five dollar bill; from the Yiddish "finf" (five).
GONEF	A thief; (GONEYVA—a theft). In the Ukraine, the word was pronounced "GUNNIF." It was not a compliment to be a "zun fun a gunnif," son of a gunnif, which was later shortened in America to son of a gun. A female thief, pickpocket, or prostitute is known as a moll and combining the two words, a thief's girlfriend became a gun moll. (I had theorized that perhaps a "meidel," a girl, was the basis for moll and as a result a gun moll was really a "gunnif's meidel," but could find no justification for my theory.)
GUNSEL	U.S. slang; from the Yiddish "gendzel," a little goose. A passive, naïve, homosexual youth; further interpreted to mean an informer or a gunman.
MAZOOMA	From the Hebrew "Mizoomin" meaning cash. It's what is needed for a "schmier."

PUTZ

A penis or prick; an idiot (common usage). The word itself consists of the two letters, "Peh-Tzaddik," which were used by Jewish thieves as a slang expression for a policeman. Since the Yiddish word for the police was "politzai," it is hypothesized that "Peh-Tzaddik" was first used as a short form of "politzai" and then vulgarly referred to as "putz."

At times information for this book came from the most unexpected sources. The following interpretation for "Peh-Tzaddik" was furnished by Rabbi Billy Berkowitz of Prescott, Arizona. He informed me that one of his teachers told him that the two letters were an acronym for "Poale Tseddik" (Hebrew), a worker for justice, i.e., a policeman. It must truly have been a literate and well educated gangster who, in calling a cop a putz, would have been aware of that derivation.

SCHMIER

A bribe; to spread it around like cream cheese.

SHAMMUS	A protector or caretaker of a synagogue. The Hebrew word "shomer," plural "shomrim," means a watchman, protector or defender. (The Jewish officers of the New York City Police Department call their organization the Shomrim Society.) Assuming no knowledge of the derivation of the word, gangsters referred to cops as "shameus." Whether it came from "shammus," a protector, or from the fact that many early policemen, especially in the big cities, were of Irish descent and Seamus was a typically Irish name, I leave for you to decide.
SHTINKER	An underworld term coming originally from Warsaw; to smell or to stink. A "rat" or one who "sings" to the cops.
SMACK (English)	Cocaine; from the Yiddish "schmeck," to smell! That which goes up your nose.
ZHLUB	A yokel, a boar or a dumb ox.

SHTINKER

An underworld term coming originally from Warsaw; to smell or to stink. A "rat" or one who "sings" to the cops.

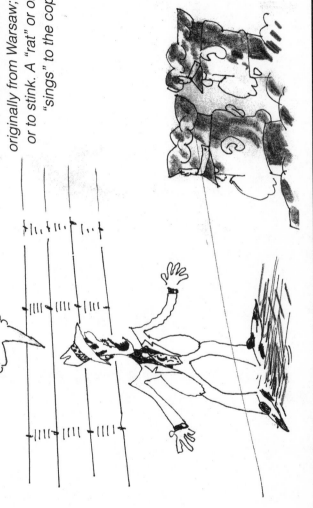

Family, Friends and "Nuchshleppers" (Hangers On)

Held together by the glue of motherhood, Jewish derivation stems, halachically (according to Jewish law), from the mother. It is the mother, who in literature and in life, ruled the home. To paraphrase the lyrics of "Fiddler on the Roof," it was the momma who had to cook and clean and sew and above all, raise the children, while the papa was either a student or a tradesman, and only rarely depicted as the dominant parent.

The overriding role of women in Jewish life is reflected in the amount that has been written about them. Strangely enough, the son and the father never came in for the praise or the criticism that was heaped upon the Jewish woman.

Going back to the Eastern European immigration to America, the pejorative term for a Jewish girl was not a "Jewish American Princess" but exactly the opposite, a "ghetto girl." These working class women, with their unrefined tastes and often vain personalities, were the constant topic of essays, advice columns and cartoons.

As the years passed, the "ghetto girls" married and had children. Family income increased, the children became educated, and the tenements of the lower East Side in New York gave way to "uptown," the "west side," and ultimately the suburbs. Mama continued to rule the roost but included in her activities were now card games, mah jongg, the country club, carpooling, and all the other manifestations of increased wealth and good living.

The lifestyle of the Jewish family was always the subject matter of both literature and theater. The reader could sit and play out the drama in his or her mind and the theatergoer could watch it played out by others.

Early immigration, sweat shops and bitter family life were reflected vividly by Sholem Asch in UNCLE MOSES. The dysfunctional Jewish family was then depicted by Henry Roth in CALL IT SLEEP, Philip Roth in GOODBYE COLUMBUS and PORTNOY'S COMPLAINT, and by Neil Simon, particularly in his BRIGHTON BEACH TRILOGY.

If it isn't enough to pick on the mothers, every Jewish family also had friends or relatives who, behind their backs, were quietly referred to as "nuchshleppers" (hangers on). Quietly is the important word because it really meant, "Sha, di kinder zoln nisht heren;" (Quiet, the children shouldn't hear) that Uncle Sid can't make a living, Tante Sarah is pregnant again, etc... In those days, many of the children knew and spoke Yiddish and after all, the children didn't have to know everything. (In my family, my parents used Russian when they didn't want us to understand.)

All that can be asked, then, is that in reviewing the words and expressions in this chapter, readers will be reminded of the happier and more humorous aspects of their own lives amidst family, friends, and "nuchshleppers."

FAMILY

TATE / MAME	Father / Mother
ZUN / TOCHTER	Son / Daughter
KINDER	Children
KINDERLACH	Lots of little ones
FETER / MUME, TANTE	Uncle / Aunt
KUZINE / SHVESTERKIND	Cousin
BUBBE / ZAYDE	Grandma / Grandpa; what wouldn't the Bubbe and Zayde do for the …
AINIKLE / AINIKLACH	Grandchild / grandchildren
CHUSEN / KALEH	Groom / Bride
M'CHATONIM	The relationship between the parents of the bride and the parents of the groom. There is no English equivalent; however, we simply say the "in-laws." Under any condition, when I see their side of the family, I know ours is better.

AYDEM / SHNUR   Son-in-law / Daughter-in-law

MISHPOCHA   The whole damn family.

AINIKLE / AINIKLACH

Grandchild / grandchildren.

FAMILY STUFF THAT WE CAN'T DO WITHOUT

BAR MITZVAH / BAS MITZVAH	Ceremony of a child's induction, at age 13, into Jewish congregational life.
BENTCHN LICHT	Blessing of the candles that kindles the Sabbath.
BRIS	Circumcision
CHASENE	Wedding
CHUPPAH	Bridal canopy
LEVAYEH	Funeral
MINYON	The ten men who say "Kaddish," the prayer for the dead, during the "shiva" period.
SHABBOS	The weekly celebration of the Sabbath.
SHIVA	The mourning period of seven days after a funeral.
SIMCHA	Happy event

YARMULKE / KIPPAH	A skull cap; a covering for the head of a male during religious services and at all times for an Orthodox Jew.

A SONG FOR THE "AINIKLACH"	LITERAL TRANSLATION
Patshi, patshi, kichelach	Clap hands, clap hands, cookies
Mame koifn shichelach	Mama will buy shoes
Tate, koifn zekelach	Papa will buy socks
A gezunt dir in di bekelach	And health in your cheeks.

And last but not least …

EIN HORA	An evil eye; do you remember the big red bow on the baby's carriage? No evil eye would dare be cast on such a beautiful kid (even if he looks like the milkman).
KINNAHARA	Said universally by those who don't really know what it means. Actually it is a squeezing together of the words "Kein Ein Hora" meaning no evil eye.

CHUSEN/KALEH

Groom / Bride

HOLIDAYS THE FAMILY CELEBRATES

ROSH HASHANNAH	New Year
YOM KIPPUR	Day of Atonement
SUCCOTH	Autumn festival of thanksgiving commemorating the desert wandering
SIMCHAS TORAH	The joy of the Torah and the beginning of a new cycle of Torah readings.
SHAVOUS	Celebration of the spring harvest and the revelation of the Ten Commandments at Mt. Sinai.
CHANUKAH	Festival of Lights celebrating the rededication of the Temple in the year 165 B.C.E.
PESACH	Passover; celebrating the exodus from Egypt.
TISHA B'AV	Ninth day of the month of Av; commemoration of the destruction of the Temples.

FRIENDS AND "NUCHSHLEPPERS"

ALTER KOKKER   An old shitter; a crochety old man.

BEHEYME   An animal; an ignorant person.

CHOCHEM /   A wiseman; sarcastically, a stupid
  CHOCHMA   person or one who makes a stupid
                remark / A wise remark or a joke.

FARBISENE   An embittered person.

FRESSER   One who stuffs himself with food,
                especially when he or she comes to
                your house.

GRUBBER YUNG   Literally, a fat youngster; one who is
                crude and vulgar.

GOY   A gentile.

KHAZER   A pig; a selfish person.

KIBITZER   An onlooker at a card game, a
                chess match, mah jongg, etc. The
                kibitzer won't play the game himself,
                but always knows when you are
                wrong. As a result, he or she is
                generally asked to keep their
                mouth shut.

MISHPOCHA

The whole damn family.

KLUTZ	A clumsy, awkward person.
KVETCH	Literally, to squeeze; or a complainer.
LANGER LOKSCH	A long noodle; a tall skinny kid.
MENTSCH	Simply translated, a person; but to be called a "mentsch" is a compliment. In a recent edition of the *Forward*, it was reported that Sports Illustrated, July 12, 1999, in a survey of their 20 favorite athletes of the 20th century listed Sandy Kaufax as number 1. Sports Illustrated stated, "He always put team before self, modesty before fame, and God before the World Series. (He sat out game 1 of the 1965 World Series because it coincided with Yom Kippur). Truly the definition of a "mentsch."
MIESKAYT	An unattractive or homely person, usually referring to a woman.

LANGER LOKSCH

A long noodle; a tall skinny kid.

MOMZER	A bastard; a tricky conniving person. If you're talking about a child, it can even be a term of endearment and is then often reduced to a diminutive, "momzerl."
NEBBISH	A shy person; a loser, a nerd.
NUDNICK	A pest; a bore or a nuisance.
PASKUDNYAK	A loathsome or horrible person. When speaking of a child, it can mean a troublesome kid but not a bad one.
PISHER / PISHERKE	One who urinates. / A kid who is wet behind the ears.
SHADCHEN / SHADCHENTE	A matchmaker, male. / A matchmaker, female.
SHIKSA / SHAYGITZ	A non-Jewish girl. / A non-Jewish boy.
SHLEMIEL	A foolish or unlucky person; a born loser.
SHLEP	To pull or to drag; a tired and slovenly person.

SHLIMAZL	One of the most interesting words in Yiddish because it comes from two different languages: "Shlim" from the German, meaning bad and "Mazl" from the Hebrew meaning luck. The shlimazl is the one over whom the "shlemiel" pours the soup. That's bad luck.
SHLUMP	A slob who hangs out with a "shlep."
SHMEGEGGE	(Origin unknown) One who speaks nonsense; an idiot.
SHMENDRIK	A fool; a stupid person. Hangs out with a "shlep" and a "shlump."
SHNORER	A moocher, a cheapskate, a bargain hunter.
SHNUK	A timid, ineffectual person.
SHTARKER	A strong person; also referred to sarcastically as a blow hard.
SHTICK HOLTZ	A piece of wood; a person with no personality.

SHVITZ / SHVITZER	A steam bath or a sauna. / One who sweats but also one who is an eager beaver.
TROMBENIK	A ne'er do well; a bum; one who toots his own horn (trombe—trombone).
TSATSKE / CHACHKE	A plaything; a toy. / A trinket or bric-a-brac. But when Mama says that sonny's girlfriend is a "richtike tsatske" (a real plaything), it isn't a compliment.
TZADDIK	A holy person, a doer of good deeds.
VILDE CHAYA	A wild animal; how a child behaves in someone else's house.
YENTE	A female mixmaster, involved in everybody's business.

WORDS AND EXPRESSIONS THE FAMILY USES WHEN TALKING ABOUT OTHER MEMBERS OF THE FAMILY, FRIENDS, AND NUCHSLEPPERS

AF TSELOCHES	Af tse lehakhes (Hebrew); to do out of spite.
A GEZUNT DIR IN KUP	Health to your head; a good wish to a student.
AIN KLAYNIKEIT	A small thing; no big deal.
ALIYAH	Emigration to Israel.
AVADA	Absolutely; when said sarcastically, you can be sure it won't happen.
AVAIRA	Sin.
AZOI?	Is that so?
BALABUS / BALABUSTA / BALABATISH	(Hebrew) Bal ha bais, head of the house; the boss / The boss lady; the real head of the household / "Mentchy"; well done; with leadership.

BASHERT / BASHERTE(R)	Predestined; inevitable. / One who is meant to be (feminine and masculine).
BETH DIN	House of laws; a Jewish court.
BISL / A BISL UN A BISL MACHTA FULN SHISL	Little / A little and a little makes a full plate.
BIZ HUNDERT UN TZVANTSIK	Until a hundred and twenty; a wish for long life.
BLITZ	Lightning; a quarterback rush in football; no score for your opponent in gin rummy.
BRONFN	Booze.
BUBBELEH	A diminutive term of endearment for a child.
BUBBE MAYSE	A grandmother's story; an old wives' tale; an unbelievable tale. Derived from the Bobe Buch (book) published in Italy in 1507 by Elia Levita which tells the story of the fantastic adventures of Prince Bovo. The unbelievable adventures became known as "Bobe Mayses," and had nothing to do with grandma (Bubbe).

BIZ HUNDERT UN TZVANTSIK

Until a hundred and twenty; a wish for long life.

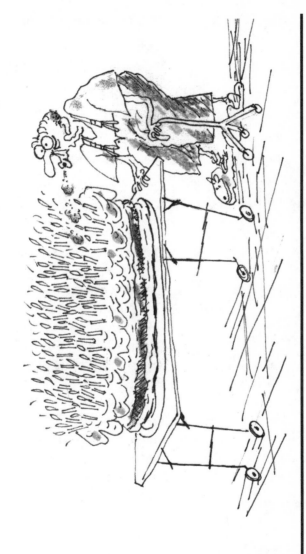

BURTCHEN	To grumble or to complain.
CHAI	(Hebrew) Numerically 18; life; root of the expression, "L' Chaim."
CHANUKAH GELT	Play money for the children, sometimes chocolate, wrapped in gold foil.
CHEDER	Religious school for young boys.
CHOZZERAI	From a pig; junk; something not wanted or needed.
CHUTZPAH	Nerve; gall; a popular book by Alan Dershowitz; a kid who kills his parents and throws himself upon the mercy of the court because he is an orphan. One striking example was heard on "Good Morning America" when Charles Gibson was interviewing Antonio Banderas who had just directed his wife, Melanie Griffith, in the movie, *Crazy in Alabama*. Gibson commented that Banderas had used Griffith's mother, Tippi Hedren, in a bit part. Banderas replied that his mother-in-law's scene had been cut and she was no longer in the picture. Gibson replied, "Boy, that is chutzpah."

DAFKE	Necessarily; in spite of.
DAVEN	Pray.
DREYDL	A game played by children during the eight days of Chanukah with a spinning toy engraved with Hebrew letters meaning "a great deed happened here."
DYBBUK	An evil spirit; when referred to a child, meaning one who is irascible; an imp.
EFSHER	Maybe.
ESSEN / FRESSEN	To eat / To overeat or to stuff yourself.
ES VET HELFN VI A TOITN, BANKES!	It is as helpful to a dead person as would be the applying of "bankes!" ("Bankes" were heated cups applied to the body to bring blood to the surface.)
FARBLONJET	Confused or lost in a maze.
FARKLEMPT	Depressed; choked up.
GAN AIDEN	Garden of Eden.
GAY VAYS	Go know; how can one be expected to know?

GENUG SHOIN	Enough already.
GESHMAK	Tasty.
GEVALD	Oh boy; a to do; a hoo-ha; a repercussion. (No English translation of "gevald" appears in Weinreich's Yiddish/English dictionary.)
GEZUNT / GEZUNTHEIT	Health / Healthiness; a blessing after a sneeze. The equivalent of "God bless you."
GEZUNT UN SHTARK	Healthy and strong.
GLITCH	To slide; to ice skate; and in modern terminology, a computer error.
GOLEM	In literature a clay figure created by a rabbi to ward off evil. Describes a person who is a lump.
GOTKES	Underwear; humorously, long underwear.
GREBTZ	Belch.

HANDL	To deal in or to negotiate.
KABBALAH	Jewish mysticism.
KABTZN	A poor person.
KANEH	Enema; for one who is in dire need of this remedy, a "Kaneh mit matzoh mehl" (an enema with matzoh flour) is prescribed. Unfortunately, the medical value and background of this prescription is lost in antiquity.
KILEH	A rupture.
KLUTZ	A piece of wood. An awkward or ungainly person.
KLUTZ KASHE	A stupid question asked by a "klutz."
KNIPPL	A button; a secret cache kept by a wife (the husband shouldn't know) to help out the children, to bet on the horses, to do a little shopping, etc. Probably derived from a pocketbook small enough to be hidden and held together by a button.
KREKHTZ	A sigh; a not too serious discomfort.
KRENK	A sickness.

BUBBE MAYSE

A grandmother's story; an old wives' tale; an unbelievable tale. Derived from the Bobe Buch (book) published in Italy in 1507 by Elia Levita which tells the story of the fantastic adventures of Prince Bovo. The unbelievable adventures became known as "Bobe Mayses," and had nothing to do with grandma (Bubbe).

KVELL	To enjoy; to get pleasure from.
KVETCH	To squeeze or to complain.
KVITCH	A squeal or a scream.
LANDSMAN	Compatriot or neighbor from the same village or district.
L'CHAIM	To life (Hebrew), a toast. But remember the designated driver.
MAMA LOSHN	The mother tongue; Yiddish.
MAYSEH / MAYSELE	Story / A little story.
MAYVEN / A MAYVEN AF DRECK	An expert; your mother-in-law, your next door neighbor or anyone else who is a "know it all." / An expert on shit; a real know-nothing.
MENORAH / SHAMMUS	The candelabra used to celebrate the eight nights of Chanukah. / The ninth candle from which the other eight candles are lit.
MESHUGGEH / MISHEGOSS	Crazy / Craziness or insanity.
MESHUGGEH AF TOIT	Crazy as death; off the wall.
METZIAH	Bargain.

MEZZUZZAH — A religious text affixed to the door post.

MITZVAH — A good deed or a commandment.

MOISHE KAPOYER — Moses excoriating his sins (derivation unknown). Upside down; backwards.

MOYKHL (Hebrew). / ICH BIN DIR MOYKHL — No thanks / Don't do me any favors, said in a rude or sarcastic way.

NACHES / SHEP NACHES — Pride, pleasure or satisfaction / To draw (as from a well) pleasure or satisfaction.

NARISH / NARISHKAYT — Foolish / Foolishness.

NESHOMA — Soul.

NISHTGUTKEIT — No goodnik (Is there another translation?!)

NOODGEN / NOODGE — To bore or to annoy; an Anglicized version of "nudgen."

NOSHER — A nibbler with a sweet tooth.

NU?	Well? (Or as the Jewish cow said, "NUUU"?)
OY VAY	Oh, it hurts. (It can be said lightly to express a degree of disbelief or seriously to express a deep emotion. "Oy vay iz mir," Oh, it hurts me, personalizes it.)
PARNUSSEH	A job or a livelihood.
PATSCH / SHMAIS	To smack / To spank.
PATCHKE / UNGEPATCHKED	To daub, smear or be messy / To dress sloppily, be overly made up or overly adorned. To over-decorate with excessive "chachkes" (knickknacks).
PAVULYA	Take it easy.
PLATZ / PLATZN / VER TSEPLATZED	Place or location. / To burst; to crack or to explode. / To tell someone to bust a gut.
SAIKHEL	Sense; mental acuity.
SEDER	The Passover meal at which the story of the Exodus is told.
SHAITL	A wig; more specifically worn by orthodox women after marriage.
SHANDA	Shame.

SHAYNA PUNIM	A pretty face. (When grandma grabs the baby and squeezes the kid's face and says, "Oy, aza ...")
SHIKKER	Drunk.
SHLOFN / FARSHLOFN / GAY SHLOFN	Sleep. / Sleepy, i.e., "farshlofene oigen" sleepy eyes or sexy eyes. / Go to sleep.
SHMAYCHL	Smile.
SHMENDRIK	A fool or a nincompoop.
SHMOOZE	To chat or to gossip; Anglicized version of "shmues." (A discussion.)
SHMUTZ / SHMUTZIK	Dirt or garbage. Believe it or not, a recent nail polish shade from Revlon! / Dirty.
SHNEID	Cut; beat your opponent in gin rummy without the opponent scoring a point.
SHNOZZ	A shortening of schnozzle; right on the schnozz; on the nose, exact or on time.
SHNOZZLE	From the German meaning snout or nose.

MAYVEN

An expert; your mother-in-law, your next door neighbor or anyone else who is a "know it all."

SHOLEM ALEICHEM	Peace be with you; a Yiddish "hello" to which the response is "Aleichem Sholem." (Unto you, peace.)
SHPILKES / SHPILKES IN TUCHES	Nails / Nails in your backside; you can't sit still.
SHPITZ	The tip or the point.
SHPRITZ	Spray (from a hose or from a perfume bottle.)
SHTETL	The town or the village in the old country.
SHTINKER	Stinker.
SHTUM	Mute.
SHVARTZ	Black.
SPIEL	From the German, spielen; to play or to ramble. In English, to talk glibly, or a salesperson's patter. In Yiddish, "shpiel" is a play (see Show Biz) or to play a game (Ich shpiel in kurtn;) I am playing cards.

TAKEH?	Is that so? Really?
TFILLN	Phylacteries.
TORAH / TOYREH	The five books of Moses; the Pentatench.
TOYREH IS DI BESTE SKHOIRE	The Torah is the best fabric.
TSORIS / GEHAKTE TSORIS	Trouble / Banged or chopped trouble; you've had it.
TZDUKEH / PUSHKES	Charity / The tin boxes for depositing coins for charity.
UMGLICK	Tragedy or misfortune.
UNGEBLOZEN	Angry; a sourpuss.
VER VAYST?	Who knows?
YEDER MONTIK UN DONERSHTIK	Every Monday and Thursday. Used to describe someone who lets days go by before he does what he should. By coincidence, Monday and Thursday are the days the Torah is read in the synagogue. I could find no relationship between what appears to be irresponsibility on one hand, and reading the Torah on the other.

YESHIVA	Elementary and high school for religious children.
YICHES	Pedigree or lineage.
YISKOR	Period of remembrance after death.
YONTEF / DER TSVAITER TUG YONTEF / A GUT YONTEF	The Yiddish pronunciation of "Yom-Tov." (Holiday) / The second day of the holiday; an old custom resulting from the inability of Jews in exile to be precise as to the exact evening upon which a holiday began. Humorously referred to one who is a "nuchslepper" or a hanger on but not really needed. / A holiday greeting; have a good holiday.
YORTZEIT	Yearly commemoration of the death of a loved one.
YU, YU, NAYN, NAYN	Yes, Yes, No, No . . . maybe.
ZETZ	A punch or a shove.

FAMILY TOGETHERNESS

No story portrays the unity of husband and wife better than the tale of Jake and Manny, both successful manufacturers in the garment center, always in competition with each other, but always good friends. Jake's wife Sally (it used to be Sara) and Manny's wife Sadie were also good friends, but loved nothing more than seeing how one could outdo the other.

Afraid that Sally might hear the news from someone else, Jake came home one evening and announced that he and Manny had each taken a mistress. Sally was devastated by the news. "Manny I can believe, but you Jake?" she questioned. "Well you know how we are always in competition," Jake replied. "When I learned that Manny had a mistress, I had to have one too." "So who are they?" Sally asked. "They're both chorus girls in the new burlesque that's playing downtown," Jake said.

To Sally, the question now became: how could she get the better of Sadie? In order to do so, there was one thing she had to know. "Jake," she said, "Tu un di hoisen (put on your pants), we're going to the burlesque."

As the chorus girls came on stage, Sally asked Jake, "Nu, Jake, which one is Manny's?" "The third one from the left," Jake answered. Sally studied the attractive young lady and said nothing. A minute or two later, Sally asked "And yours, Jake, which one is yours?" "The fifth one over," he replied.

After watching the girls do their routine and dance off the stage, Sally turned to Jake and with a big smile said, "You know what, Jake, unsers is shener." (Ours is prettier.)

What greater devotion can there be than between father and daughter? When Rosalie came to her father and announced her forthcoming marriage to an actor on the Yiddish stage, Papa was less than enthusiastic.

"I don't care how handsome he is or how well he speaks Yiddish," Papa said. "A living he'll never make and you will be unhappy."

Finally, in an attempt to console his daughter, who was miserable and angry at him, Papa said, "All right. Let's go to the theater and I'll meet your young man."

After watching the show, Papa turned to Rosalie and said, with a big smile, "Rosalie, you have my permission. Kenst chasseneh hubn mit im." (You can get married to him.)

Rosalie was overjoyed. "But, Papa," she said, "What changed your mind?"

"Rosalie," he replied, "he looks like a fine boy. He is handsome and I'm sure he has a good personality. But one thing I know."

"What's that?" asked Rosalie.

"Kein actior is er nit," (An actor he isn't), replied Papa.

FAMILY CURSES

ZOLST ZICH SHMADEN A TUG FAR DEM VEN
MESHIACH KUMT.
You should convert to Christianity a day before the Messiah comes.

ZOLST CHASENEH HOBN MIT ROTCHILD'S TOCHTER
A TUG FAR DEM VOS ER VERT BANKRUT.
You should marry Rothschild's daughter a day before he
becomes a bankrupt.

A CHULERIA ZOL DIR TREFN.
Cholera should strike you. ·

ZOLST VAKSN VI A TSIBBELEH, MIT DEM KOP IN
DRERD UN DI FIES ARUF.
You should grow like an onion with your head in the
ground and your feet in the air.

MEH ZUL DIR AROISRAISN ALE TZAINER ACHUTZ
AINZ UN AF DEM ZULST DU HOBN A TZUN VAITIK.
They should extract all your teeth but one and in that one
you should have a toothache.

ZOLST VAKSN VI A TSIBBELEH MIT DEM KOP IN DRERD UN DI FIES ARUP.

You should grow like an onion with your head in the ground and your feet in the air.

Slang, Curse Words, The Anatomy and other "Shmutzike Zachn" (Dirty Things)

A number of years ago, when I lived and practiced law in New York, an old friend and client who was a literary agent, called and asked if I could write a dirty book in Yiddish (transliterated, of course). I asked him what he had in mind and he sent me copies of two dirty books, one in French and one in Spanish. Believe me when I tell you, they were dirty.

After a few days of review and consultation with others, I called him back and told him that it was my belief that Yiddish did not lend itself to this kind of book. Between us, what I meant was not a whole book; but certainly a chapter. After all, we know that YOU CAN'T DO BUSINESS (OR MOST ANYTHING ELSE) WITHOUT YIDDISH. Wouldn't that include dirty business, as well?

Any language that is said to be complete with its own grammar and a voluminous literature must also have slang, curse words and expressions that describe that part of life that the parents say is "nisht far di kinder" (not for the children). But as long as it's for the adults, let's go.

BAYTZIM	(Hebrew) literally, eggs; balls or testicles.
BUBKES	Goat droppings; of little or no value.
COK IM UN	Shit on him.
DRECK / SHTICK DRECK	Shit; manure. / A person referred to as a piece of shit.
FAGEL	A bird; a homosexual.
GAY IN DR'ERD	(Contraction of der erd) Literal translation: Go in the earth. What you really mean is, go to hell.
ICH HOB DIR IN DR'ERD	I have you in the earth (literal). I have you in hell.
KNISH	A tasty dish (see FOOD). / A woman's sex organ.
KURVE / KURVISHE SHTICK	A whore or a prostitute. / Whorish behavior.
LOCH	A hole. A woman's vagina.
LOKSCH	Noodle; a slang expression for an Italian, a pasta eater.

MOMZER

Bastard; used at times to denote someone who is shrewd and clever but more often describes your boss, your partner or anyone who doesn't have your brains or ability, but makes more money than you.

PULKES /
GRUBBE
PULKES

(See Food.) The thighs of a "zaftig" (well endowed) lady. / Even more than just pulkes; in this case, fat pulkes.

PUTZ / FUTZ /
ARUMFARTZN

A penis or a prick; more aptly used to describe a stupid person. / A corruption of putz meaning to fool around. / To fart around or to waste time.

SHLANG

Snake; penis; a contemptible person.

SHMO

An alternative for "shmuck;" an idiot or a fool.

SHMUCK /
SHMECKLE

In German it means jewelry. In Yiddish it has come to mean a penis or a prick; thereby relating the same to the family jewels; interchangeable with putz or shlang. / A diminutive "shmuck."

SHTUP	To push; to screw (have intercourse).
SHVANTZ	A jerk; a person who behaves stupidly.
TRENEN	To fornicate.
TSATSKE / TSATSKELE	A hot number; a bimbo. / A diminutive, pretty little girl with "shticklach" (cute, sexy affectations).
TSITSKES / GROISE TSITSKES	Mammaries; tits. / Oh boy, big tits.
TUCHES	Backside; rear end; ass.
GRUBBER TUCHES	A fat ass.
A SHTICK TUCHES	A piece of ass.
KISH MIR IN TUCHES	Kiss my ass; trying to settle out of court.
PATSCH IN TUCHES	A slap on the ass.

TUCHES AFN TISCH	Put your ass on the table; stop skirting the issue and get to the point; results; an unintentional or humorous corruption of a now rarely used expression, "tachlis afn tisch" (results on the table).
TUSHY	A slang Americanization of "tuches."
YACHNE	A gossip; a coarse or vulgar woman.
ZETZ	Intercourse; to screw.

"SHMUTZIKE MAYSEHLACH" (Dirty Stories)

What else do the ladies talk about during Mah Jongg but their husbands? But not Mildred. "Zi zitst vi a shtume." (She sits as if she is a mute.)

"What's the matter, Mildred?" they ask. "Your husband doesn't satisfy you anymore?"

This went on for weeks, and finally Mildred, not able to stand the questioning or the ridicule, replied, "Jake couldn't get it up so he went to a specialist who suggested that Jake have an operation."

"Takeh (really), an operation," the ladies said. "What kind of operation?"

"Monkey glands," said Mildred.

"Monkey glands?" chorused the ladies. "Nu, have things gotten any better?"

"Worse," said Mildred.

"Worse, what could be worse?" asked the ladies.

"Now, every night," said Mildred, "when it's time to say good night, "kricht er arain in bet, est bananas un kratzst zich in tuches." (He crawls into bed, eats bananas, and scratches his ass.)

✿ ✿ ✿ ✿ ✿

MONKEY GLANDS

When his son found out that Papa was going to marry his secretary, who was even younger than himself, he insisted that Papa visit the family doctor for a talk about having sex with a much younger woman, preserving his strength, his health, etc.

Finally Papa came out of the doctor's office and the son asked him whether he understood everything the doctor told him.

"Absolutely," Papa replied.

"And you asked him about having sex at your age?"

"I did," Papa answered. "But there is one thing I'm not sure of."

"And what is that?" asked the son.

"Zug mir vifl mol a vakh" is semi-annual? (Tell me, how many times a week is semi-annual?)

Two rabbis were discussing the announcement that appeared in the newspapers of the forthcoming marriage of Marilyn Monroe to Arthur Miller.

"It won't last a year," said one of the rabbis.

"Aza yor af mir," (such a year on me) replied the other.

A new "mohel" (a performer of ritual circumcisions) came to the "shtetl" and in an attempt to make his presence known, rented a little shop and painted his name and occupation on the window. Fearing this would not get enough attention, he hung a big clock outside the door.

Along came one of the townspeople who asked the "mohel," considering that which he did for a living, why he hung a clock outside of his shop.

"Vos den zol ich hengen?" (What then should I hang?) asked the "mohel."

Yiddishisms
and
Englishisms

Part I of this chapter goes back to the riddle of which came first, the chicken or the egg? Was it a Yiddish expression translated into English or was it the other way around? I don't know the answer and I don't know where to find the answer. So you decide.

Part II of this chapter is a reversal of the rest of the book. We will sample some well-known English expressions and see how they turn out in Yiddish. The interesting aspect of these expressions is that they are said one way in English, are totally differently in Yiddish, yet both have, basically, the same meaning.

PART I

ABI GEZUNT

As long as you have your health. (It is an excellent sign off when someone concludes a long and heart-wrenching story which you had no interest in hearing, so you say, "Nu, abi gezunt.")

AF ALTZ DING IS ER A MAYVEN

As to all things, he is an expert.

AZ MEH LEBT, DERLEBT MEN

If you live long enough, you'll live to see everything.

AZOI GAYT ES

So it goes.

AZOI VERT DOS KICHEL TSEBROKHEN

That's how the cookie crumbles.

BAYS DIR DI TSUNG

Bite your tongue. (Pray it doesn't happen.)

DOS EPPL FALT NISHT VAIT FUN BOIM	The apple doesn't fall far from the tree.
ES OIS DOS HARTZ	Eat your heart out. (Be jealous; see if I care.)
FREG NISHT	Don't ask.
FUN DIEN MOIL BIZ GOT'S OIERN	From your mouth to God's ears.
GAY REKHEN	Go reckon or go figure (it out).
ICH DARF ES VI A LOCH IN KOP	I need it like a hole in the head.
KUK NOR VER S'REDT	Look who's talking.
MACH A LEBEN	Make a living.
MAZL TOV	Good luck.
MAZL UN BROCHA	Luck and blessing.
MEH KHAPT MER FLIGN MIT HONIG VI MIT ESIG	You catch more flies with honey than with vinegar.
ME ZOL NISHT VISSN DERFUN	You shouldn't know from it.

SHA / SHVAIG SHTIL	Keep quiet / Shut up.
TZVISHN UNDZ GEREDT	Between us; confidentially speaking.
VI IS ES GESHRIBEN?	Where is it written?
VOS VAINKER MEH REDT, IZ BESER	The less you say, the better.
ZAI GEZUNT	Be well.

PART II

A poor workman blames his tools.
"Az a meidl ken nit tantsn, zogt zi az di klezmer kennen nit shpiln."
If a girl can't dance, she says the band can't play.

Don't jump to conclusions.
"Khap nisht di lokshn far di fish."
Don't grab the noodles before the fish.

Don't talk nonsense. Don't bust my chops.
"Hak mir nisht kein chainik."
Don't knock my teapot. (Derivation unknown.)

Easier said than done.
"Es tut zich nit azoy laikht, vi es redt zich."
It doesn't happen as easily as it is spoken.

I couldn't care less.
"Es ligt mir in linkn pyate."
It is lying in my left sole.

If everyone threw their troubles into a pot, they would all take their own troubles back.
"Ainer vaist nit dem anderns krenk."
One doesn't know the other's sickness.

Don't talk nonsense. Don't bust my chops.
"Hak mir nisht kein chainik."
Don't knock my teapot. (Derivation unknown.)

Man proposes, God disposes.
"A mentsch tracht un Gut lacht."
A person thinks and God laughs.

Money makes the world go around.
"Az men hot di matbaieh, hot men di daieh."
If you can pay, you have the say.

One doesn't see one's own shortcomings.
"Af zich zait men nisht dem hoiker."
On yourself you do not see the hump on your back.

Talk, talk, talk, don't you ever shut up?
"Vos is afn loong is afn tzoong."
What is on your lung is on your tongue.

There is no such thing as a perfect person.
"Alle meiles in ainem iz nita bei kinem."
All virtues in one (person) do not exist in anyone.

To bribe; to pay the piper; to cross one's palm.
"As me shmirt, fort men."
If you grease (the wheels), you travel.

To cut off one's nose to spite one's face.
"A nekame af di vantzn ven dos hoyz brent."
(It is) revenge on the bedbugs when the house burns.

You can't sit with one "tuches" on two chairs.
"Me ken nit tantsn af tzvai chasenes mit eyn mol."
You can't dance at two weddings at the same time.

You can't take it with you.
"Takhrikhim macht men un keshenes."
Shrouds are made without pockets.

With friends like you, who needs enemies?
"Hit zikh far di fraynt, nit far di faynt."
Guard yourself against your friends, not your enemies.

When you laugh, the world laughs with you; when you
cry, you cry alone.
"Ven du lachst, yeder zait; ven du vainst, kainer zait."
When you laugh, everyone sees; when you cry, no
one sees.

Law
and
Politics

n the heat of litigation, tempers often flare and lawyers sometimes have difficulty expressing their frustrations. When English fails, Yiddish may come to the rescue.

So it happened that defense attorneys arguing a recent summary judgment motion in federal court in Boston wrote, in a responsive pleading, "It is unfortunate that this Court must wade through the dreck of plaintiff's original and supplemental statement of undisputed facts."

The plaintiffs' attorneys, not to be outdone, responded with a motion that could double as a primer on practical Yiddish for lawyers. The outcome is not known.

UNITED STATES DISTRICT COURT
DISTRICT OF MASSACHUSETTS

MONICA SANTIAGO,
    Plaintiff,

    v.

SHERWIN-WILLIAMS CO.
Et.al.
    Defendants.

Civ. No. 87-2799-T

Plaintiff's Motion to Strike
Impertinent and Scandalous
Matter

Plaintiff, by her attorneys, hereby moves this Court pursuant to Rule 12(f) of the Federal Rules of Civil Procedure to strike as impertinent and scandalous the characterization of her factual submission as "dreck" on page 11 of Defendant's Rule 56.1 Supplemental Statement of Disputed Facts (a copy of which is attached hereto as Exhibit A). As grounds therefore, plaintiff states:

1. For almost four years now, plaintiff and her attorneys have been subjected to the constant **kvetching** by defendants' counsel, who have made a big **tsimmes** about the quantity and quality of plaintiff's responses to discovery requests. This has been the source of much **tsoris** among plaintiff's counsel and a big **megillah** for the Court.

2. Now that plaintiff's counsel has, after much time and effort, provided defendants with a specific and comprehensive statement of plaintiff's claims and the factual basis thereof, defendants' counsel have the **chutzpah** to call it "**dreck**" and to urge the Court to ignore it.

3. Plaintiff moves that this language be stricken for several reasons. First, we think it is as impertinent to refer to the work of a fellow member of this Court with the Yiddish term "**dreck**" as it would be to use the "sibilant four-letter English word for excrement." Rosten, *The Joys of Yiddish* (Simon & Schuster, New York, N.Y., 1968) p. 103. Second, defendants are in no position to deprecate plaintiff's counsel in view of the **chozzerai** which they have filed over the course of this litigation. Finally, since not all of plaintiff's lawyers are **yeshiva buchers**, defendants should not have assumed that they would all be conversant in Yiddish.

   WHEREFORE, plaintiff prays that the Court put an end to this **mishegoss** and strike "**dreck**."

KVETCHING

by defendants' counsel.

William Rogers, the Secretary of State for the United States, visited Israel at the time Golda Meir was Prime Minister. The one request that Rogers had was that he be allowed to pray at the Wailing Wall. Golda was more than pleased. She furnished him with a yarmulke and, accompanied by Secret Service from both the United States and Israel, proceeded, with him, to the Wall.

Upon arriving, Rogers appeared to be somewhat uncertain as to procedure, but being ashamed to ask, he turned to the Wall, raised both hands and cried out, "Oh, God, let the Israelis give back the Sinai; Oh, God, make the Israelis return the Golan Heights to the Syrians; Oh, God, tell the Israelis to withdraw from Lebanon."

Hearing these prayers, the head of the Israeli Secret Service who was standing next to Golda, said to her, "Madame Prime Minister, do you hear what Secretary Rogers is saying?" Lighting up another cigarette, Golda laughed and said to her bodyguard, "Zorg zich nit, er redt tazum vant (Don't worry, he's talking to the wall.)"

One of the ministers in Prime Minister Golda Meir's cabinet, while preparing her for a visit from Secretary of State Henry Kissinger, informed the Prime Minister that Mr. Kissinger considered himself an American first, Secretary of State second, and a Jew third. Without hesitating, Golda replied, "Bai mir is gut; ich layn from rechts biz links." (It's okay with me; I read from right to left.)

Index

Biographies

LEON H. GILDIN, a lifelong resident of New York, graduated from law school in 1950 and was immediately drafted into the U.S. Army. After a two-year hitch (18 months in Germany), he was discharged and upon his return to the U.S., was admitted to practice in New York. Despite the need to make a living practicing law, Mr. Gildin got involved in show business and for more than forty years, was retained as counsel to many actors, writers, and composers. He was also involved in the night club business as producer of shows in the Latin Quarter and the Playboy Club. He produced both on and off Broadway and has worked with authors in the development of scripts and musical material for the stage.

In addition, Mr. Gildin acted both as an attorney and as a principal in the development and optioning of properties for major motion pictures. He has further been the executive producer of a number of television documentaries, the most recent of which *Theresienstadt, Gateway to Auschwitz: Recollections from Childhood*, received a Blue Ribbon Award from the American Film and Video Festival and is sold in the United States Holocaust Memorial Museum in Washington, D.C., and the Museum of Tolerance in Los Angeles, California.

Most recently, Mr. Gildin has turned to playwrighting while continuing to keep busy with putting deals together for both films and TV.

During all of this time, Mr. Gildin remained active in the Jewish organizational world. He was a member of the Board of Trustees of the Sholem Aleichem Educational Foundation, Chairman of a branch of the Farband Labor Zionist Order, counsel to and Chairman of the Executive Committee of the Jewish Teachers Seminary—Herzliah Hebrew Teachers College and was an active participant in the Yiddish Vinkl of Great Neck, N.Y.

Mr. Gildin is now retired and residing in Sedona, Arizona.

✽ ✽ ✽ ✽ ✽

PAUL PETER PORGES, born in 1927 in Vienna, Austria, is a renowned American cartoonist and humorist. In 1939, prior to the outbreak of World War II, Porges left home at the age of 12. He spent the war years in France fleeing the Germans and in 1944 fled illegally into Switzerland and safety, where he was accepted at the Ecole des Beaux-Arts in Geneva. He studied fine art from 1944 to 1947 and then emigrated to the United States, where he finally rejoined his parents, both survivors of German concentration camps, and his brother, who had served with the U.S. Army in the war.

Within three years following his arrival in the United

States, Porges was drafted into the army where his cartoons appeared in *Stars and Stripes* and the *Army Times*.

Upon rejoining civilian life, Porges studied at the Cartoonists and Illustrators School, now known as the School of Visual Arts, in New York City. About 1954 he began selling cartoons to the *Saturday Evening Post*, and soon thereafter, Porges's cartoons began appearing in *Playboy*, *The New Yorker*, and MAD magazine. His work for MAD lasted for some two decades during which he published four books of MAD cartoons and two scholastic publications in the field of art and cartooning.

Paul Peter Porges is presently a member of the faculty of the School of Visual Arts in New York City and was honored in 2000 with a retrospective exhibition of his work at the Jewish Museum in Vienna, Austria.

Also available from Hippocrene Books . . .

English-Yiddish/Yiddish-English Practical Dictionary
Expanded Edition
Romanized
David C. Gross
   • over 4,000 romanized entries
   • appendix of idiomatic expressions and proverbs
   • appendix of common Yiddish words used in the English language
4,000 entries • 146 pages • 4¼ x 7 • ISBN 0-7818-0439-6 • $9.95pb • (431)

Hebrew-English/English-Hebrew Dictionary & Phrasebook
Israel Palchan
   The special feature of this dictionary and phrasebook is that it includes
the original Hebrew along with easy-to-use pronunciation for English
speakers. Along with a dictionary of 2,000 entries, phrasebook chapters
cover all aspects of daily life. This guide is ideal for travelers to Israel.
2,000 entries • 180 pages • 3¾ x 7 • ISBN 0-7818-0811-1 • $11.95pb
• (126) • Fall 2000

Hebrew-English/English-Hebrew Conversational Dictionary
Newly Revised
David C. Gross
   This concise and popular dictionary is indispensable to the traveler in
modern Israel or anyone seeking an introduction to the ancient language
of the Bible. Its 7,000 entries are Romanized and accompanied by helpful
hints on pronunciation and communication, allowing the reader to begin
using the language right away.
7,000 entries • 157 pages • 4¼ x 7 • ISBN 0-7818-0137-0 • $9.95pb • (257)

Hebrew-English/English-Hebrew Compact Dictionary
David C. Gross
   • over 7,000 entries
   • Easy-to-read format
   • Handy conversational reference
7,000 entries • 157 pages • 3 x 5 • ISBN 0-7818-0568-6 • $7.95pb • (687)

Ladino-English/English-Ladino Concise Encyclopedic Dictionary
(Judeo-Spanish)
Dr. Elli Kohen & Dahlia Kohen-Gordon
   This unique book is the first Ladino dictionary for English speakers!
Ladino, also known as Judeo-Spanish or Judezmo, was the language

spoken by the Sephardic Jews who settled in the Ottoman Empire after their expulsion from Spain in the 15TH century. Definitions for the words include the origin, the cultural context of expressions and their usage, making the book an invaluable reference tool for anyone interested in Romance and Oriental languages and Jewish culture.

8,000 entries • 602 pages • 5½ x 8½ • ISBN 0-7818-0658-5 • $19.95pb • (742)

Dictionary of 1,000 Jewish Proverbs
Compiled by David C. Gross

This multilingual collection of 1,000 Jewish proverbs is extracted from the rich oral traditions of Hebrew, Yiddish and Aramaic, and has been edited with both the scholar and the general reader in mind. Covering a wide range of topics, the proverbs reflect lives whose spiritual abundance often contrasted a material impoverishment.

"A new friend is like new wine—you drink it with pleasure."

These sayings were compiled from many sources including the Bible and the Talmud as well as Jewish proverbs from other lands. The wisdom, clarity and wit of these proverbs ring true to present-day life.

Over 400 subjects are listed in alphabetical order. There are special markings in the margin denoting the language of origin for each proverb.

125 pages • 5½ x 8¼ • ISBN 0-7818-0529-5 • $11.95pb • (628)

Treasury of Jewish Love Poems, Proverbs & Quotations
In Yiddish, Hebrew, Ladino and English
Edited and transliterated by David C. Gross

Evocative words of romance and passion have been gleaned from the Bible, rabbinical sources, medieval scholars and modern poets. Among the authors included are Bialik, Ibn-Gabriol, and Halevi. Original works appear in Hebrew, Yiddish and Ladino alongside their English translations. This lovely gift volume includes 44 poems of love and 70 quotations and proverbs.

127 pages • 5 x 7 • ISBN 0-7818-0308-X • $11.95hc • (346)

Also available as an audiobook:
The Hebrew portion of the cassettes is read by Noya Einav, an Israeli actress and radio personality. The Yiddish portions are read by Suzanne Toren, an actress with Broadway credits and experience as a radio and television announcer and narrator. The Ladino portion is read by Saul Yousha, an actor whose mother tongue is Ladino. English translations are read by Ken Kliban, an actor with Broadway credits and extensive narrating experience.

Audiobook: 2 cassettes • ISBN 0-7818-0363-2 • $12.95 • (579)

Hebrew Love Poems
Edited by David C. Gross
Illustrated by Shagra Weil

Although much of Hebrew poetry has traditionally focused on the religious and philosophical, the theme of love has remained vivid throughout the centuries of Jewish life. This beautifully illustrated book of over 90 love lyrics translated from the Hebrew is a celebration of this enduring theme.

Ranging from *The Song of Songs* to poetry from modern Israel, there are poems of praise and devotion, of quiet reflection, joyous celebration, carefree humor, and sensuous beauty. Shagra Weil's delicate, evocative illustrations are the perfect complement to the works they accompany.

91 pages • 6 x 9 • illustrations • ISBN 0-7818-0430-2 • $14.95pb • (473)

Jewish First Names
Edited by David C. Gross

This addition to Hippocrene's *First Names* series includes over 1,300 Jewish first names for boys and girls in Hebrew, Yiddish, Aramaic and various European languages. This charming gift edition gives the origin and etymology of each name as well as nicknames. The book includes new name forms like Davida or Davidine—"beloved" (feminine versions of David) as well as traditional names like Raphael—"God has healed."

126 pages • 5 x 7 • ISBN 0-7818-0727-1 • $11.95hc • (90)

1,301 Questions and Answers About Judaism
David C. Gross

Now contains a new chapter on trivia: "Famous and Notable People." Already updated for the new millennium, *1,301 Questions and Answers About Judaism* also addresses issues in today's headlines:

- How do rabbinical rulings address the debates on abortion and artificial insemination?
- Is an intermarried family eligible to join a synagogue?
- Are chemical additives kosher?

A Book-of-the-Month Club selection, the first edition drew much acclaim:
"A kaleidoscope vision of the rich heritage of Judaism."
—Rabbi Norman Lamm, President, Yeshiva University
"A reliable guide to the ways of Judaism."
—Professor Seymour Siegle, Jewish Theological Seminary of America
"Ideal for busy people seeking ready answers on the basic questions . . . the amount of information packed into this one volume is amazing."
—Rabbi Alexander Shindler, Union of Hebrew Congregations

This comprehensive volume contains Questions and Answers about the history and basic tenets of Judaism, for practicing Jews, as well as for newly-observant Jews, and for non-Jews seeking a deeper understanding of Judaism.

373 pages • 6 x 9 • ISBN 0-7818-0578-3 • $17.95pb • (678)

Under the Wedding Canopy: Love and Marriage in Judaism
David C. and Esther R. Gross

This comprehensive book delves into the wide range of marriage customs, ceremonies, traditions and practices that have become a part of the Jewish heritage for nearly four thousand years. David C. Gross, America's premier author of Jewish works, and former editor of *The Jewish Week* (New York), and his wife, Esther, have spent years assembling material that will shed new light on the vast, complex world of Jewish marriages.

"An ideal gift for couples . . . practical, full of useful information."
—The Forward
"Jewish wedding customs from around the world . . . advice on how to create a happy marriage."
—American Jewish World
"A portrait of Jewish marriage that is unfailingly positive and unabashedly traditional."
—Na'amat

243 pages • 5½ x 8½ • ISBN 0-7818-0481-7 • $22.50hc • (596)

Israel: An Illustrated History
David C. Gross

Despite its physical size, Israel from the earliest times to the present has always been a major player on the world stage. The birthplace of Judaism, which in turn became the mother religion of Christianity and Islam, Israel holds a very special place in the minds and hearts of hundreds of millions of people, particularly in the Western world. This concise, illustrated volume offers the reader an informative, panoramic view of this remarkable land, from biblical days to the 20TH century. Since its foundation a scant 50 years ago, Israel has emerged as a veritable magnet and spiritual resource for Jews and Gentiles alike. With topics exploring art, literature, music, science, politics, religion, and more, this is a wonderful gift book for travelers, students, or anyone seeking to expand their knowledge of Israeli history, culture and heritage.

148 pages • b/w illustrations/photos/maps • 5 x 7 • ISBN 0-7818-0756-5 • $11.95hc • (24)

The Jewish People's Almanac
Revised Edition
David C. Gross

Here is the revised edition of this perennial favorite, a compendium of little-known facts and illuminated insights on the history of the Jewish people.

Before Steven Spielberg even started filming the Academy Award-winning *Schindler's List*, David C. Gross had already recounted the heroic story of Oskar Schindler in *The Jewish People's Almanac.* In this upbeat and offbeat almanac, you will meet the likes of Harpo Marx, a Yiddish-speaking FBI agent, and Sammy Davis, Jr., writing about his conversion. In addition, you will read about Hanukkah in a monastery as well as a Jewish view of homosexuality. Humor, anecdote, and historical fact all have their place in this treasury of Jewish lore.

"Wonderful stories abound."—Publishers Weekly
"Laugh, enjoy and learn."—Jewish Chronicle

596 pages • 5½ x 8½ • ISBN 0-7818-0288-1 • $16.95pb • (372)

Why Remain Jewish?
David C. Gross

One of America's premier authors tackles the number one issue facing the American Jewish community—the large number of young Jewish people, teens and young adults, who are abandoning Judaism and the Jewish community. The high rate of intermarriage—now exceeding 50% of all marriages involving American Jews—along with the significant number of Jews who convert to another religion, missionary sect or cult, has caused a widespread feeling of dismay and sorrow throughout the Jewish community.

Why Remain Jewish? presents a wide range of arguments, facts and figures, and historical and contemporary insights designed to reverse the current trend. The book shows young people that Judaism is a religion and a way of life that brings fulfillment and serenity to its practitioners, and adds a meaningful dimension to their lives; and that being Jewish is a glorious, lifelong commitment to intellectual growth and ethical insight. Includes a glossary of Hebrew terms.

"He shares practical information for getting involved in Jewish life."
—The Jewish Week

171 pages • 5½ x 8½ • ISBN 0-7818-0216-4 • $9.95pb • (213)